God, My Mom, and I

Copyright © Tracy R. Eleazer

ISBN: 978-1958186-05-3

Publisher, Editor and Book Design:

Fiery Beacon Publishing House, LLC

Fiery Beacon Consulting and Publishing Group

Graphics: FBPH Graphics Team, Dashona Smith

God,
My Mom,
And I

Tracy R. Eleazer

Table of Contents

The Dedication

The Introduction

The Journey to Survive

The Start of the Journey

Testing Days

Final Results

The Family Meeting   **25**

Hair Loss Day

Rough Days

Drawing Near

The Dedication

I want to dedicate this book to my Granddaughter Ja'Miya aka Nu Nu. My mother, your "Nannie Peanut" adored you and you were light of her life. You gave her a second chance of life to be able raise a little girl all over again from birth to seven years old. There was not anything that she would not do for you and would never allow anyone to hurt you. Your Aunt and Uncle couldn't eat any of the snacks she had put up for you. You were everything to her, she loved you, and she knew you loved her.

She would sacrifice and take you to work with her knowing it was dangerous for you to be around those hot dry-cleaning machines. You would ride the city bus with her to get your nails done, and hers too, starting at the age of two. (Now because of her you keep your nails done.) Your Nannie took her last breath once she heard your voice, your laughter in the room. She waited for you, she waited to hear from her Nu Nu. Your Nannie Carrie made a promise to **your Nannie Peanut that she would always take care of you; I made that promise also as she laid in transitional state that I would take care of you too.**

The Introduction

My name is Tracy R. Eleazer, and I am writing this story about my mother's battle with Breast Cancer. She faced many battles throughout her life, but she would always survive and in my view, this would be no different.

My Mother had me when she was fifteen years old, my grandmother passed away when my mother was nineteen; I was only three years old at the time of her death. My mother lost custody of me because my family felt that since my grandmother passed away my mother was not going to be able to take care of me. Prior to my grandmother's passing, she requested that if anything was to ever happen to her, she wanted her sister, which was my great-aunt, to take care of me. Of course, my great-aunt honored her request.

Throughout the years I would visit my mother. My dad would come to visit me at my great-aunt's house whenever he would find out where my mother was living. He would take me to go see my mom; we kept it a secret because we did not know if my great-aunt would be upset with my dad about it. We thought if she found out she probably would have stopped my dad from taking me with him. I would be so happy to see her as I remember, but sometimes I would go years without seeing her. I never got upset or felt angry about it. All I wanted to do was see her.

As time went on by, my mother started visiting me more often - by this time I was ten years old. She started dating this man name Herberto. My mother's life was looking different in a good way. Eventually, my great-aunt felt that my mother was in a better position to take care of me, so she made a hard decision and allowed me to me to go live with my mother again. I was so excited! I could not wait to get packed up so I could go live with her. Once I got to my mom's place (where she lived with Herberto), I got myself unpacked and I was starting to get settled into my room. The first day that I was there, my mother walked to the corner store but I stayed at the apartment until she came back. Once she left, Herberto asked me to come into their bedroom. I sat on the bed wondering why he wanted to me to come into their bedroom. Herberto went into his dresser drawer and pulled out sock full of coins. The sock looked heavy, but that was about to be the least of my worries. He then asked me to let him see my breasts and said that he would let me have the sock full of coins if I did. I replied "No!" I was surprised that I could even muster a reply being that I felt numb, confused, and scared. I could collect my words to tell my mother - I didn't know how. As time went on, things got worse. My mother and I were abused by the hands of Herberto for many years, but thankfully, one day we got a way. That's another story to be told.

As I share my mother's journey, I pray this story will reach the heart of those who have and are battling Breast Cancer, this awful deadly disease that is taking lives of so many family members. Early detection is the key in order to fight this disease and to survive. Unfortunately, my mother did not survive, my heart was broken. It is still broken. I miss her dearly, but through it all, it was God My Mom and I.

The
Journey to
Survive

THANKSGIVING 2014

My mom told me she felt a lump in her right breast. I felt it, but it wasn't big. My mom had Breast Cancer before in her left breast in 2009 but only had to do radiation treatment five days a week. Thank God, she was cured and healed and the lump was small and did not require her to receive chemotherapy treatment. Since she was a prior Breast Cancer patient, she was supposed to get follow-up visits once a year, but the clinic she attended closed, so she did not have a doctor to go to for her regular mammograms. She was not eligible for Medicaid because she was not on disability. You had to be considered disabled through Social Security Administrative before you can qualify for Medicaid. For anyone who does not understand the process, it can be a winding road to endure.

My mom was able to get into a clinic to be seen for regular health evaluations. She had advised her doctors that she felt a lump on her breast; an appointment was supposed to had been scheduled for her, but it wasn't. Months went by with no resolve. One day, my mom broke out into a bad rash that seemed to have no rhyme or reason and was all over her hands, her face, her arms, legs, and her hair. She would itch so bad, and even when they gave her different antibiotics, creams, and ointments to help relieve the discomfort, nothing worked. To make matters worse, the type of insurance she had would not cover for her to be seen by her dermatologist, and so she had to pay for those appointments out of pocket. She worked part-time and she really could not afford to pay for the visit out of pocket, but she did the best she could.

One day I was at work when she called my phone crying bad because she was so irritated by the rash but had run out of medication. Without hesitation, I left work and went to go get her prescription; my dad, helped me pay for it. It never mattered what I was doing or what I had going on, if she called me needing me, I stopped everything to go see what was going on with her; she is my mother and I had to do what her only child knew to do and that was to take care of her.

My Mother was feisty and strong! No matter what she was going through she would fight her way through it. Once I got to her and rubbed the cream on her and gave her the medication, she felt better and laid down to rest, but even after going back to work, I checked up on her throughout the day to make sure she was still feeling better. Some days she would be okay, and some days were still hard for her. We never knew why she had the rash, but it eventually cleared up. She did have some scars and sores because of the intense itching she endured, but like everything else, she made it through.

The Start of The Journey

JUNE 6, 2015

My mom finally got an appointment scheduled to have her mammogram at the Women's Hospital. I know she was nervous, but she just wanted to make sure that she was okay. She had the test done. We just waited on the results.

There is something about the moment when you take the test and all you can do is wait. Time went by so slow, as we embraced every moment we had with her. Every sound to us was the sound of a phone ringing or some kind of notification that none of us could verify that we even wanted to hear. The tick tock of the clock echoed in our hearts as we waited for the final results.

Testing Day

My mom had to have more tests done while getting the results of her x-ray and scans and blood work. We had been at the Breast Cancer Center all day seeing different doctors. My mom was getting agitated because she was tired, ready to get the results and go. The results came back, and on that day my mom was diagnosed with Stage-3 Breast Cancer. The room was silent, so silent that you could hear a pin drop. She started to cry and there was nothing I could do to erase the pain she felt in that moment. I could not afford to cry because I had to be strong for her; I had to be her voice. In this newfound strength, I began to ask questions and answer questions so she could fully understand what is going on.

According to the x-ray the lump was big. The Oncologist felt Chemotherapy would be the best treatment to shrink the tumor, and later, she would have surgery to have the breast removed. After my mom heard the news, she did not want to speak to any more doctors; in the meantime, more tests were performed to make sure the Cancer did not spread to any other parts of her body.

Final Results

My oldest daughter Diesha went with my mom to her appointment to get the results of all the additional tests that were run. The Oncologist told my mom the Cancer had spread to other parts of her body, specifically to her lungs, bones, and brain. It goes without saying - she began to cry even more. We were then told that only radiation treatment could treat the brain, and that the treatment would not affect any other parts of the brain. Aggressive Chemotherapy treatments were needed as soon as possible. Diesha had recorded the visits so I could hear what was being said because I had to work. It was in that meeting and in what seemed like a whirlwind of time, that the doctors re-diagnosed her with Stage-4 Breast Cancer. At some point before she went to the doctor to confirm the lump, she felt and I strongly believed that she knew she had cancer and now that thought had become her reality.

The
Family
Meeting

I called the family to come over to my mom's house for family meeting to let them know what was going on. Her brothers and sisters came over along with my cousins. Diesha and I told them what the doctor told us earlier that day. My mom's oldest sister Mary began to cry. She told my Aunt Mary that she would be alright she just has to go through the treatments. She sat there in silence for a moment, and then broke down; she cried so bad. At first, I didn't know how to comfort her, so I just sat beside her and put my arm around her. At that moment I felt hopeless; I didn't know what to do.

She finally stopped crying and decided to take a walk outside; my Uncle James went outside with her, and they started walking down the sidewalk to talk. I am not sure what was they talked about, but the love they shared was evident. Despite the hurt we felt, none of us were willing to disturb the moment they shared – that was their moment, and we did not know how many more of those moments they would be permitted to create. Everyone started to go home, as it was getting late. Once they left, it was just my mom and I sitting there quietly. I can't say how she was feeling but I could see the hurt and disappointment on her face.

Radiation Day

JULY 31, 2015

My mom went to have the radiation treatment for the spot on her brain. Only one treatment was needed to treat the spot and she did pretty good receiving the treatment, too. Even though the Cancer had spread to other parts of her body, her Cancer was still listed as Breast Cancer because that was the main cause of her having Cancer. Tears and all, we as a family positioned ourselves to have her back one step and one cancer at a time.

August 4, 2015

1stChemotherapy Treatment

To prepare for her chemotherapy treatments, my mother was prescribed some cream to numb the area where the port was put in on her right side of her chest. She had to put the cream on two hours before treatment so she would not feel any pain while she received the treatments. Once I got to her house to take her, she was already dressed and ready to go in her "Living Pink" t-shirt! As we got in the car, I asked,

"Mom, are you okay?"

She looked over at me and said, 'I'm fine, just ready to get it over with." We arrived at Wesley Long Regional Breast Cancer Center, where she had to get registered. She had blood work done first, then had to see the doctor before receiving treatment. This consisted of getting her weight check and blood pressure, filing out more paperwork, and getting prescriptions ordered for nausea meds, pain meds and whatever other medications she needed. At this appointment, they also provided other resources that were available for her to receive such as financial assistance with her light bill and rent etc.

We were given a buzzer that would go off whenever it was time for her to be seen for lab work, office visits and treatments. While we waited for the buzzer to go off, she would work her crossword puzzles or play a game on her cell phone. I would be on Facebook or playing Candy Crush.

The buzzer goes off.

Through the doors we go, walking down the hallway to the treatment room. We walked into the room where there were other patients receiving treatments too, thirty-three beds total. This was my first time seeing a treatment room, to see other patients in that room getting chemotherapy treatments was breath taking. No one would ever imagine that so many people would be found in the same space fighting the same monster. They were hooked up to multiple IV bags, some were on oxygen, nursing staff was full, and some people were even sitting alone while receiving their treatments. I can't imagine how many different types of cancer encompassed that room; it was completely overwhelming to see it and to know that my mother was not the only one fighting to survive. The area my mom had to receive treatments was a small area that only had room for one person to sit with her. She had to sit in a recliner while I sat on a small bench. There was just enough room for our stuff.

There was also a personalized tv in her area so she could watch whatever she wanted to. Sci-fi and Lifetime, The Young and The Restless and The Bold and the Beautiful were her favorite shows to watch so I knew without questions what shows the day would bring. The nurses came to administer the chemotherapy drug through her port. Treatment lasted for more than one hour. Once the medicine was all gone from the IV bag, they flushed her port, cleaned it, and put bandages on the port so it would not get infected. Then, left the treatment room to go home.

We sat outside on the bench that is near the front entrance, waiting for valet parking attendant to bring my car. As we were sitting, I heard my mom say with her feisty self,

"I don't know what she is looking at me like that for!"

I turned my head toward my mom to see what she was talking about and noticed my mom smoking a cigarette. I replied, "Ma what are you doing? I would look at you like you are crazy too for smoking a cigarette right in front of the Cancer Center! 80% of the patients here have cancer from smoking cigarettes! You couldn't have waited until we got in the car or when you got home to smoke?" She then explained that she was nervous because it was her first treatment. We laughed about it once we got home because I knew she was ready to go off on somebody. I had to think about what she was feeling, her emotions were on high. She needed something to calm her nerves down and I had to respect that.

Acceptance

My mom felt that the cancer was going to take her out and she made it known. She would often say,

"I'm going to live my life and not let cancer get me down."

I know deep down in her heart she wished she didn't have it. The doctors decided to take my mom out of work, and Lord knows, she hated that. She worked at several dry cleaners' locations throughout her life, more than twenty years, since I was ten years old. When she first started working at the dry cleaners, she would walk to work from The Grove that was on the Eastside of town, to High Point Road on the South side of town. Eventually, she was able to get rides back and forth to work from her co-workers and would pay them gas money every week for taking her back and forth to work each day.

Now that she was out of work, she always had to have something to do. She would change her living room around and her bedroom at least once a week. She would move that furniture around all by herself just to say that she accomplished something and to keep her mind off of what was happening in her body. I am sure that she may have heard an ear full about that, but her heart was determined and her persistence, far greater than her circumstance.

Regardless of the size, you better believe that her family was there for it all. She lived in a one-bedroom apartment but none of that mattered because we still had all the holidays at her house. She loved to have family and friends over, and her apartment literally became the hang out spot. We would be packed up in her apartment as if it were mansion, from the front porch, the living room, and her back yard.

She would cook every Sunday; she made the best canned collard greens and green beans. She would tell me what ingredients she would use and how to cook them, but I never paid attention, I was just ready to eat. I would go to her apartment every Sunday after church to eat dinner. I would fall asleep on her couch and feel her putting a blanket over me every time. She would tell me to go get in her bed to stretch out, but I insisted on just staying on the couch curled up in a corner. I miss those days.

Hair
Loss Day

August 8, 2015

My mom called me early that Saturday morning while I was at work and said that while combing her hair, it began to come out. This was not just a normal "shedding," but instead it was coming out in big chunks. As was the norm for us, the moment she called anything I was doing stopped. Time stood still as I listened to my mother share the depths of her heart with me. Even as we spoke, tears fell and neither one of us fought it away.

My work schedule consisted of me working on Saturdays. It was ironic how I was working Monday through Friday, until my mother got sick. As soon as we received the news, my scheduled changed, and I began working Tuesday through Saturday. I hated working on Saturdays. It was getting to the point that I had to depend on other people to take her to her appointments. That part was stressing me out a little bit, because it was difficult getting doctors reports from others instead of me hearing it all for myself. I feel that God already knew what was going to on with my mom, and that my scheduled was changed to Tuesday through Saturday so that my Mondays would be free and open for me to take her to her scheduled doctor appointments. I did not miss any of appointment she had.

That Saturday when I got off work, I went to go see her and she had her hair in zip lock bag. Fresh out of tears, she asked me if I wanted it. I told her that I could not take it, not at that moment. A friend of her shaped her hair up for her after the hair loss she experienced. I am grateful for that safe space that she was granted – a space to release every emotion she felt as her hair fell to the floor. She looked so cute with her hair being cut short. I will never forget the smile that came across her face when I told her how beautiful she looked. I thought she looked – priceless and renewed! My mom's hair meant everything to her and everyone knew it. She always kept her hair done, but in one moment, all of that changed. If I had to tell her one million times or more that she was beautiful, I was more than willing to do so. She was the most beautiful woman I had ever seen in that moment and I was proud to call her my mother.

Rough
Days

AUGUST 16, 2015

As I was getting ready for church, my mom called me crying saying she had a bad headache and that she could not see anything. The only thing that she was able to see was my phone number on her phone. Without hesitation, I rushed over to her house so I could take her to the hospital. When I got there, she was sitting on the couch rocking back and forth and moaning and groaning because she was in so much pain. Every emotion I wanted to let out, did not have permission to happen, not in this moment. She needed the strongest version of me that I had available, and I was determined to be what she needed in that moment.

When we arrived at the hospital, I advised the receptionist she was a Stage-4 Breast Cancer patient. I got her registered; we waited less than five minutes before a nurse came and got her. When we got to the back room, the nurses gave her an IV and pain meds. She was only able to get the IV in her left arm, as my mom had bands on her right arm to alert the nurses that they could not take blood or insert an IV in that arm. The medicine she was given relieved the pain and, eventually, she went to sleep. While I was there, my Uncle James came over to check up on her, too. The nurses stated that the chemotherapy gave her the migraine.

39

While I was upset with the explanation, I was just grateful that they at least had one. Thankfully, she felt better once I got her home and settled. I stayed with her to make sure she was okay.

August 18, 2015

My Hair Cut Day

I decided to cut my hair short and close to support my mom losing her hair and needless to say, I felt so honored to do so. Every act of support that was in my control, I was more than willing to oblige and this, to me, was simply another expression to make her smile and remind her that she was not by herself in this fight. I called her to tell her that I had a surprise for her. Once I got to her apartment, I walked in the door she said "Girl, you cut your hair off," and I replied,

Yep, to support you!

I did whatever I had to do so she would not feel alone. I stood right by her side, I refused to go anywhere, and she knew it.

August 24, 2015

Complication day

My mom had to have a treatment but this day proved to be unlike the rest as we ran up on a complication - the nurse was unable to get blood out of her port. Moments like this made me even more grateful for walking this road with her. Once they told me what was wrong, I instructed the nurse that she would need to lay my mother on her right side. I then told them that she would have to lay flat and cough. Once that happened, I knew that the blood would flow, enabling her to get her treatment. I thank God I was there because it could have gone a way that was deemed totally unnecessary to everyone in the room, especially my mom.

September 14, 2015

I remember this day – it was so long! She had an early morning appointment. This was different for us being that her appointments would normally be in the afternoons. She had to have lab work, see the doctor, and have treatment. Her appointments were on Mondays for two weeks followed by one week off. She did fairly good getting her treatments and we did not experience nausea or weight loss. She was afraid that she was going to experience those side effects but she didn't, thank God. She ate normally and never lost her appetite. Smiling as I type, reminiscing on how she would make her some homemade pinto beans and homemade cornbread just to prove the point! She loved drinking buttermilk. Whenever she would ask for it or if I just wanted to treat her, I would go to Bo' Jangles, get her a biscuit and a small bowl of pinto beans. She loved eating it. She loved eating Honey Buns and trust, anything she wanted she got it.

My Aunt Mary would come and stay a few days with my mom to make sure she was okay. She wouldn't cook for my mom, because quite frankly, my mom didn't like her cooking! She would say "Mary can't cook," with that sassy and unforgettable tone.

My Aunt Mary and my mom were very close. My Aunt Diana was next to the baby sister, my Aunt Pam. My Aunt Diana passed away at the age of forty from heart disease and needless to say, we were so devastated. She was the first sibling to pass away. She had two children, Alex and Meosha. I was so hurt and broken for a long time when she passed away. Her loss seemed so unfair - she loved the Lord she did not miss church for anything. She was always praying and worshipping the Lord. Their bibles were marked and highlighted with different bible verses and chapters. She would insert Alex and Meosha's names into a lot of the scriptures.

There were six kids. My grandmother had two boys and four girls. My Uncle Tight is the oldest. He was really close to my mom and they saw each other just about every day. They would fuss at each other all the time, but they were always together. My Uncle James is the baby brother. He was there for my mom and I whenever I needed him to be. He didn't hesitate to come visit my mom at the hospital or come sit with her while I had to go run an errand.

My Aunt Pam would catch the city bus to my mom's house to sit with her too and watch tv. She always made sure my mom had a cellphone to use. My Aunt Pam had her one-year wedding anniversary in my mom's backyard. Just like I mentioned before everything was always at my mom's house so the house stayed full of memories. Family just being there meant the world and I believe that even when she didn't say it, our being there gave her strength that she did not even know she had.

October 16, 2015

More Testing

Mama had an MRI on her brain to see if the cancer tumor had shrunk. She had to go to the imaging center, and as she went, we prayed and trusted God for a good report. I was able to take the day off so I was able to go with her to the appointment. While we were there waiting for her to be seen, the changing room had some yellow slip resist socks they gave her to put so she would not slip while walking to the testing area. They sold themselves with their see-through packaging and everything! My mom and I laughed about taking a few pair of the socks, no lie! After my mom was finished with her MRI test, the nurse asked us if we wanted an extra pair. We laughed about the thought of us going to take an extra pair as if we had not already planned it in the back of our heads. Instead of us having to plan and go forth with "the great escape," the nurse gave it to us anyway. My mom was mess of laughter, but it was worth it to see her smile.

October 18, 2015

Another Bad Day

Early one Sunday morning, my mom was not feeling well. Without question, I went to church early that morning to pray for her. I had to stand in the gap for her. I had to have strength for her when she did not have it for herself. I believed God for healing of her body, no questions asked. I would spend the night at my mom's house and I would fall asleep in her bed with her refusing to leave her side. I had to make sure that she was okay. I would give her pain medicine whenever she would be in pain and listened out for every moan, groan, or request. This night I stayed with her, and she said:

"Lord, I wish I had a new body.

I heard her and could barely collect my breath to reply. She couldn't deal with the pain. She said, "I can deal with the cancer, but not the pain." I can't say that I remember her every saying that with her previous battle. Regardless, all I could do was breathe, and yes, be strong.

MRI
Results

October 21, 2015

We got the results from the MRI and the lab work. Thankfully, the results showed the tumor on her brain was not getting any bigger and the tumor in breast was shrinking. The chemotherapy was working!

My mom was hoping they were going to tell her the cancer was gone and upon hearing the update, looked a little disappointed. She was disappointed, but I was praising God because for me, even this piece of improvement was only a glimmer of the healing to come! I told her to be happy that the treatment is working, but my words went in one ear and out the other. I knew deep down in her heart that she wanted it to be gone completely. I know I would've wanted it gone too, but in that moment, I just wanted to give her something to fight for though I knew that her fight was diminishing. She was tired of dealing with the pain and constantly going through all of that she was going through. She had another chemotherapy treatment scheduled for the October 26th and I knew that she was dreading it.

The Turnaround!

October 25, 2015

My mom really started to feel bad but today, I attended church as usual. I have been a member of my church for over twenty years. I would pray, sing, listen to the word and pay my tithes and offerings.

My Uncle James invited me to this church, and I've been a member since. They knew exactly who he was once I told them I was related to him and that I was his niece. I normally would not talk to anyone but instead, just leave right out of the door. On this day, I felt the urge to talk to a few members of the church and was embraced with open arms. The members of the church were willing to come and sit with my mom or whatever I needed. I felt so relieved once I opened myself up to them. I needed all the support I could get because my mom was starting to change, it wasn't looking good and I didn't know how much more I could take.

October 26, 2015

I arrived at my mom's to take her to her appointment, but when I got there, she wasn't dressed as usual. My Aunt Mary said she had been in bed all day sleeping. She was weak, and she didn't understand me. I had to help her get dressed and put on her shoes and coat.

She didn't look good at all.

She looked vastly different.

She wasn't right.

I was able to get her to the car. Once I got her to the Cancer Center, I had to push her in the wheelchair because she couldn't walk on her own. Once we got in, she was registered. When I ran into her nurse and she took one look at my mom, she knew that something was wrong. She knew my mom would have been alert and talking but today she was not doing any of that but instead, looked dazed and confused. The nurse asked her for her name she hesitated to answer; she also asked her what month it was but she could not respond and instead, just looked confused.

Without a doubt, the nurse felt that my mom needed to be admitted immediately. She rushed her to the other side of the hospital. Once they got her settled, it was determined she had pneumonia and had a fever. I stayed at the hospital with her all night long to make sure she was okay and that her fever was getting under control. She slept all night long as she was giving a higher dosage of pain medicine. I did not understand how things changed for her so fast. Just two weeks ago, she was walking and talking on her own and now this? She even had to have a catheter put in since she couldn't get up to use the bathroom on her own. I just didn't understand why or what was happening. It was like a light switch flicked and every changed for her.

October 28, 2015

More of my family members came by to see my mom. She was prayed over with anointed oil and was downgraded from ICU status. She was finally able to eat and was talking and laughing with everybody. This day was a good day for her and I thanked God for the turn around.

The next day came and it was as if the previous day never existed as she went back downhill again. I figured she over did herself, or that maybe the visits were too much for her. As a result, I had to limit her visitations and she had to take breathing treatments, because she had COPD as well. She remained in the hospital for about one more week. After that good day, she didn't have any more good days like that. It was a up and down battle. At this point I was starting to accept the fact that my mom wasn't going to be here too much longer. Despite my deepest and heartfelt prayers, I had to surrender to God's will, and whatever that entailed.

November 4, 2015

My mom was discharged from the hospital, and I took off work early so I could pick her up and get her home. I had to pick up my Aunt Mary first so she could be with my mom while I worked. When we got to her room she said, "There is Andy and Gumb, what took you so long?!" She was ready to go and I didn't blame her. This time she came home with an oxygen tank and breathing treatment supplies and a shower stool. Once I got her back home and settled in, I had to go back to work. I got off work and went back to her house to get her prescriptions filled. While I was at Walmart, an employee was sitting on the bench with her feet all propped up talking on the phone, and no one was able to sit down. Regardless of how long I've been in church, my facial express always tell what I am thinking. She noticed my facial expression, so she moved her feet and sat up straight, but I decided not to sit down because her feet were on the bench. I ended staying at Walmart for almost two hours waiting to get everything filled. That situation could have gone another way, but my mission was bigger than her taking up a whole bench.

Once I was done, I had to give her breathing treatments. Diesha came over to help me. She was pregnant so she really couldn't do much. We would both change her and dress her making sure she had everything she needed before we would go home. Every day when I would get off work, I would go see her to check in. Some of her medications were too big for her to swallow so I would have to crush them up in a pill crusher mixed with applesauce; this was the only way she was able to take her medicine.

We tried to get an in-home aid to come in to take care of her during the day, a friend of the family knew somebody that was willing to come by to sit with my mom and make sure she was taking care of, but once my mom saw the lady she was like "No I don't want her in my house messing with my stuff and going through my house being nosey." We had other options, but I felt that they were not sincere about helping, they were just in it for the money, so we just took turns as a family taking care of her.

One night, Diesha was at my mom's house, I mentioned to her my mom needs a good bath. Diesha and I got everything prepared so she could take a bath. She had a walker that had a seat and wheels on it. We had to get her up out of the bed because she didn't have enough strength to walk on her own. We were struggling to get her into the seated wheelchair so we could push her to the bathroom, we had to be extra careful with my mom and Diesha because she was pregnant, and I didn't want her to push too hard and hurt herself and/or the baby. It was hard getting her out of her bedroom, but we finally made it out after we bumped into the walls and bathroom doors. We finally got her in the shower as I was getting ready to bathe her, until she yelled out "Ouch my toe!" I had stepped on her toe and didn't even realize it. As I began to wash her, she just sat there and did not say a word; she just let us take care of her. We changed her sheets, applied lotion on her and put her pajamas on. She breathed a sigh of relief- this was the silence breaker for us. I felt she knew we were trying our best to make sure she was well taken care of and even her slightest sigh was a sign of approval. I was so honored to be able to take care of her. She was my mother.

November 7, 2015

As I had heard before, being a caretaker was not easy; in fact, saying yes to this life came with the default decision to allow it to take over your whole life.

For me, a few and far between moment finally came. I went to the beach with my friends, Andrea, Sharon, Rhonda, and Nisha, but while I was away, I called to check up on my mom to see how she was feeling. My Aunt Mary and our family friend stayed at the house with her. Our family friend was always at my mom's house because they were good friends. (He shares a son with my Aunt Pam.) I had a good time at the beach, but my mom was constantly on my mind. I kept calling to make sure she was okay. I knew that I drove my family crazy, but I didn't really like being away from her like that. I always wanted to stay close to her, just in case something happened, so that it wouldn't take me long to get to her.

November 9, 2015

We were leaving the beach to come home. As I was driving, I got a call from Diesha telling me they had to call the ambulance because my mom's nose was bleeding; my Uncle James came over, too. The ambulance took her to the hospital where she ended up being admitted. Tests were run to determined what was going on with her. As to be expected, everything stopped, and we immediately got on the road to head home. The whole time I was driving my friend Andrea kept asking me if I wanted her to drive, but I told her that I had it all under control. I drove all the way home from Myrtle Beach S.C. to Greensboro N.C., and upon my arrival, immediately went to the hospital.

Diesha told me that my mom mentioned to her that she had a dream, but she would not tell her what the dream was about. I kind of figured in my heart what the dream may have been about but did not want share details either as they were too heartbreaking to imagine. Diesha, my Uncle James, and I stayed there with here in the room until Diesha left. Once she exited, my mom looked at my uncle and I and said the words my heart had no desire to receive:

"I can't keep going on like this y'all."

In a moment like that, all you can do is brace yourself, breathe and pray. Once my uncle left, I asked, "Mom, did you tell Diesha you had a dream?" "Yes," she replied. I knew that I was going to have to dig deeper to get the answers that I needed. "What was the dream about?" My mom got quiet. I continued, "Did you have a dream that you were going to die?" She replied and said, "Something like that." She wouldn't go into any more detail than that. I asked her if she was getting ready to leave me but she did not respond. As I grabbed her hand, I asked her if she wanted me to stay with her. She replied, "It doesn't matter, it's up to you." This answer was not odd to me, because she never really required me to do anything but instead would always say, "Whatever you decide Tracy." For me, that meant that I needed to be there, so I stayed.

I spent nights at the hospital with her at least four to five times during the week. I would get up early in the morning so I could take my baby girl Nadia to work and my grandson to daycare. I had to get to work myself by 8:30am so I kept a duffle bag, a pillow and blanket in her hospital room closet. I slept in a recliner chair, it was very uncomfortable, but I made it work. I would sleep in the recliner chair listening to worship music, worship music helped me sleep peacefully at night. One morning I fell on the floor as I was getting out of the recliner; I leaned forward on the foot part of the recliner - it folded down and caused me to hit the floor. It was loud too and sounded as if I had smacked the floor. My mom was asleep, but the impact of my fall woke her up. She yelled,

"Tracy!!!"

"Ma, I'm okay."

I just knew I had injured my wrist, thank God I didn't.

November 15, 2015

I called my mom after I got out of church to see if she needed anything before, I came over to the hospital to see her. She told me she wanted a Cook-Out Hot Dog, so I got it for her. She only ate half of it. Anything she wanted I made sure she got it. She kept complaining about her right-side hurting, so different tests were done to try and figure out why was she having the pain. Finally, a test was done called Thoracic Scan, which determined that the cancer had spread to her back and spine, causing the bones in her spine to rub against each other. The doctor told my mom that the cancer had spread and that she will need to follow up with her Oncologist to see what else could be done. As the doctor walked out of the room, my mom began to cry. I just sat there in silence; I really didn't know what to say. I told her that we would wait and see what her Oncologist had to say and continue to trust God. A few days later she was discharged from the hospital.

One night, we were sleeping in her room until she woke up. "How long have you been here," she asked. I replied, "Ma I've been here for a while." She responded with "OKAY" and went back to sleep. Another night I was asleep in her bed with her, she woke up talking about her job. She was telling one of her coworkers how to press shirts and she was making hand movements demonstrating how to do it in the air, and then she went back to sleep. All throughout the day and night she would be in pain and I would have to give her pain medicine. She would yell out whenever pain would hit her; she would ball up her fist and her body would jerk a little bit. It was hurtful to hear her and see her being in pain. She hated feeling that pain. She continued to say,

"I can deal with the Cancer but not the pain."

Drawing Near

November 23, 2015

We had a meeting with the Oncologist in the morning to seek what other treatment can be provided since the cancer was spreading fast. As I slept with my mother, at around 3:08am I was on social media and this video popped up. The artist was playing the piano singing this song called "Dear God." I put one of my earphones plugs in my mom's ear so she could hear the song even though she was sleep; I had the other earpiece in my ear. Despite the fact that she was asleep, I felt that she could still hear the song. It went like this:

[1]"Feels so good to make it this far, I didn't think I could take it so long.

There were days I wanted to quit, I said surely this is it, but I held on.

Lord, I thank you for my life, for every victory in you I've seen, all the moments Lord, you kept me.

So, I say thank you Lord for my life.

---

[1] "Dear God", Smokie Norf_l, 2009

If I never live to see another day, there is nothing I would take or change away.

I've had so many ups they out far outweighed my downs, Lord, I thank you for my life, for my life Lord, I thank you.

I realized some didn't make it, I could've been one of the ones who lost their way, there were times I almost went crazy but I'm still here with my life.

I thank you for my life.

I know you kept me, so I thank you for my life. I may not be all that I hoped for, you and every dreamed had not yet been realized but to see your face one day I know it's all going to be worth it.

Lord, I thank you for every mountain and every valley, everything you brought me through. I know it was you.

Lord. Thank you, Jesus, for my life!!!

I cried and cried myself to sleep feeling that my mom was going to leave me sooner than I thought. My heart was aching so bad, and I felt so heavy, that I cried myself to sleep. I woke up, I gave my mom her medicine and dressed her because we had to meet with her doctor. I had to leave to go pick up Nadia and her boyfriend so they could help me get her into the car. When I left my mom was sleep. When I got

66

back and I walked into her room, she was on the floor. I quickly ran to her aide,

"Ma, oh my GOD! What happened?"

She then explained that she was trying to get some water. She had a cup with a straw in it so she could drink water or juice by sipping it. She tried to get to it on the table that was next to her bed on the table, by herself, but because she was weak, she fell out of the bed. I don't know how long she had been on the floor like that, but after that day she couldn't hold anything in her hands anymore on her own. I would hold the cup for her. We were able to get her off the floor and onto the bed. I was so upset that she had fallen but I had to pull myself together, for her. We got my mom to the car, and we went on to the appointment. After having her blood drawn, we were given a buzzer that would alarm us when it was time to see the doctor. As soon as the buzzer went off, I pushed my mom in a wheelchair into the doctor's office. He walked in and began to tell us that the cancer had spread and that there was nothing else that could be done for her. His news stopped me in my tracks, and time stood completely still.

I said, "you mean no chemo, no nothing unless the Lord says so?"

He looked with empathy and said, "Yes. She may make it through the holidays." I felt numb and in shock and could barely process the words he has just given me. He then told me he would contact hospice, so they can start coming to see her. He then put in a request for her to receive a blood transfusion it would give her some energy.

It was so unreal to me as if I was dreaming.

I looked over at my mom but she was in a dazed-out state. Once he told me about what was going on with my mom he just walked out of the room and there my mom and I sat, still trying to determine if we had heard the same news. Another nurse came into the room to go over the medications she could and could not take from that point moving forward. As she was speaking, I asked,

"There is nothing else that can be done for my mom?"

She looked back at me and said "no."

"This is it?? Nothing?"

"Yes. Just make her comfortable as possible."

The appointment was set up so she could receive the blood on Wednesday. I took my mom home to my house so I could take care of her. I wasn't going to send her to Hospice because I did not want to miss out on anything regarding her care. One of my cousins that has experience with hospice as a social worker explained to me what was going to go on while she was under hospice care. She also advised me to contact a funeral home and give them my mom's information just in case she passed away at my home; I understood the instructions, but that broke my heart. The main thing was that I did not want her to wake up and not see me there with her. I did not want her to feel alone. I took her to my house, and I laid her on my couch, I used a blanket from her house so she could lay on top of it. I got a few things I know she needed while she was at my house. I called the family to come over to my house so I could tell them what was going on. I also called my friends to come over too so we could have prayer for her.

Diesha came over after she got off work and she walked in not knowing anything yet. I told her what the doctor said that there was nothing else that could be done and that hopefully she would make it through the holidays. She looked at me at said, "She can't have chemotherapy?" With tears streaming down my face, I found myself now responsible for delivering the same news that the doctor and nurse had delivered to me, "It's not going to help." The tears that were once mine became my dear Diesha's.

My family and friends started to arrive to see my mom as she laid on the couch. She recognized everybody which was a good sign and proof that she was still in her right mind. My heart and mind keep telling me to make sure her soul was saved. I knew it was God. My friend William came over one day. He grabbed my mom's hand and asked, "Do you know who I am?" She said, "Yes, and you still smell good!" We just laughed; every moment became precious. Afterwards, my friends began to pray. I held her hand and she squeezed my hand real tight. Anointing oil was poured on her as I cried out to the Lord and said,

"Lord save her soul!"

When they finished praying my mom said "Amen!" I saw tears running down her face. She wanted to sit up and go outside. It was dark and cold that night; she tried to stand up to walk to the door, but she fell back down because she couldn't catch her balance. She had just enough strength to sit up on the couch. My Uncle James sat next to her and held her hand while talking to her (he always knew when to show up).

I wanted to go to her apartment to get some more of her things such as her oxygen tank, more clothes, and her medicine. I also wanted to get her radio because I wanted to play gospel music for her while she was at my house. As I was leaving, my friend William was leaving too. As we stood on the front porch, I felt in my spirit that praying for her was not enough. I asked him, "Is she going to be okay?" "Yea," he replied. I felt like no more needed to be done besides ensuring her salvation. My Aunt, Uncle and my friend Angie started to leave to go to with me to my mom's house to go get her the things my mom needed. As we were leaving, William was walking to his car. He called my name and said, "We must go back in and do the prayer of salvation." When we go back into my house, my mom was still sitting up talking to one of my aunts. William grabbed her hand and asked,

"Do you believe Christ Jesus died for your sins?"

"Yes!"

"Do you accept Christ Jesus as your personal Savior?"

"Yes!"

At that moment I felt relieved to know she gave her life to the Christ. God's grace and His love her, allowed her to be alert and have enough strength to talk and understand what was being asked of her. I left to go to her apartment. As soon as I got there, I knew that she needed to be able to come back home to her own apartment; just being able to cook again her in her kitchen, would bring life to her! I began to cry. Once I said that, Angie told me that my mom's life was in a critical state and that I could not allow anyone to come by and see her. I cried even more as I loaded up the truck with her belongs. My aunt sat with her until I came back.

When I got back to my house, she was still sitting up doing okay, and was alert; she even took a picture with my Uncle James. My aunt told me when we left to go to my mom's apartment, that my mom understood what was going on. She stated my mom hadn't done anything too bad, such as killed anyone or robbed anyone that would prevent her from going to heaven. My reply was just as powerful as the charged I had received to ensure my mother's salvation:

"Your soul must be saved in order to make it into Heaven. If it's not you won't make it into Heaven."

A few of my friends came over to visit me and my mom. My cousin Jackie came over to see her as well. Jackie and my mom were really close as their birthdays are one day apart. They called each other twins. He was the only one that could mock or imitate her - he was so funny. He sat beside her and asked her who he was. The moment she said "Jackie," he started to cry and held her hand. Once everybody left, I put the other couch together so I could sleep close to her to prevent her from rolling over and falling off the couch. I got her settled, changed her diaper and gave her medicine so she could rest. That night, she told me that she did not want to be a burden on me. I looked her right in the eyes and said,

"You will never a burden to me, you are my Mother. I'm supposed to take care of you."

As she slept, I cried thinking about the truth that my mom would have to leave me soon. She was going to die at any time. This was the week of Thanksgiving and it felt like time was moving like lightning. The Hospice nurse came by and did a home visit to get everything she needed such as a bed, more diapers, and personal items. I was given a prescription to get her some morphine as it would make her comfortable. The hospice nurse gave me a booklet filled with information how to take care of her while she was at my house.

The next morning, I got my mom changed and I gave her some medicine. I told my son Quan to get her some fresh cold water with some ice in it, since I had to get signed on to work. Once he left for school my mom said to me, "Quan knows I'm dying" I asked, "how do you know?" She said, "He just knows." Then, she went to sleep. I worked from home, so I was able to take care of her and have more one on one contact with her; this also helped her to know that she was not alone. My house was familiar to her and that brought us both peace. I know for fact that I would have not been focused on work, knowing she was in a hospice center all alone and that no one she knew cared for her. On my breaks and lunches, I would give her medicine and feed her broth and/or soups, applesauce, or soft foods because she couldn't chew and swallow big chunks of food.

The next day Advanced Home Care brought the bed for my mom. I had them to put it upstairs, so she could be in private room, so she would be able to get some rest and not be exposed to all kinds of the downstairs activities. I didn't want everybody to see her sick like she was and being exposed to all kinds of germs. I only allowed close family and friends to see her. Once I got her bed made up with her pillows and covers that came from her apartment, I felt much better knowing she would be safe in a bed that had rails on it to keep her from falling on the floor. I kept the radio on in the room it stayed on 1400am so she could her gospel music all day and night. I had a tv in the room too, but she mainly slept she didn't watch tv that much, but I kept it on as well so she could watch her favorite shows if she was able to.

At night, I would hear her talking though I wasn't able to understand what she was saying or who she was talking to. One night she yelled out and said, "MARY," which is her oldest sister, then she said, "TRACY!!!" I jumped up and ran in the room to see what was wrong. She started talking about a girl that had a baby. She said, "the girl has a baby and I think she gets food stamps." I said, "Ma what girl? she said, "the girl with the baby," then went back to sleep. I fell asleep in the chair that was in the room next to her bed just in case if she yelled out again, so I could hear her. I dozed off for a little bit and I felt her tapping my pillow waking me up. She was telling me something, but I couldn't understand what she was saying. Again, she drifted back off to sleep. I didn't get much sleep at all that night; once I am awakened out of my sleep it is hard for me to go back to sleep.

November 25, 2015

She was scheduled for her blood transfusion. I asked my children to come and help me get her ready because I had to work and meet with the hospice nurse. My daughters came right over. Diesha helped get her dressed and cleaned up. Nadia purchased a baby monitor for me, so that as I worked, I would be able to hear my mom yell out if she was in pain during the day and in the middle of the night.

She also purchased some more diapers and a few other things for her. Diesha took her to the appointment for me. The hospice nurse arrived and immediately I began asking her questions.

"I don't understand what happened?! In October she was fine talking and walking doing for herself now its November she can't do for herself."

She told me that the chemotherapy attacks the good and bad cells of the body. When it attacks the good cells, it breaks the body down. She then told me that was what happened to my mom -her good cells were attacked as well by the chemotherapy. It hurt my heart to know that the chemotherapy broke her down like it did. At that moment, I felt like chemotherapy was not a good idea, because it changed her to the point she could no longer walk and do for herself. All kinds of emotions ran through my mind. I went on to work. At around 4:00 pm, the nursed called to advise that my mom was ready to be picked up and that my mom was getting restless (she kept trying to get up out of the wheelchair.) I called Diesha to pick her up; she was not answering her phone so I kept calling back-to-back. I thought I was going to have to sign out of work and go pick her up until Diesha finally answered the phone. She had fallen asleep but was on her way to get her. As she arrived, my mother said,

"What took you so long? I'm ready to go"

"I'm here now Nannie!"

My mom quickly replied and said, "My name is Sylvia not Nannie!" My mom was so funny and was always talking junk, always fussing, and just oh, so feisty. She finally made it back home, where I was able to get her settled in. I gave her some medicine so she wouldn't be in pain. Later, that night she was talking all night long off and on. When I would get up to go check on her, she would always be looking up at the right-side corner of the ceiling. She would be talking but once again I couldn't understand what she was saying.

November 26, 2015

Thanksgiving Day, I woke up early and I gave her some medicine and got her cleaned up. She told me "I talked to them people up there," as she pointed at the ceiling. I said, "What people Ma?" but she wouldn't respond. I walked out of the room for a minute and when I came back in, she was at the foot of the bed, trying to get out of the bed. "Ma where are you going?" She let me know that she was going to the bathroom that was right across the hall. She could see it from her room. I said, "Ma you can't go the bathroom you have to use your diaper." She kept trying to get up, so I gave up trying to hinder her from the attempt. I tried to see if she could walk, but she got weak again. I was hoping she was going to be able to walk to the bathroom, but since she wasn't able to, I had to put her back into the bed. Before I was fully able to put her back into bed she said. "Hand me my pants, so I can go to the store." I started laughing I said, "Ma you can't go the store," then, again, she went back to sleep.

The hospice nurse was coming for a home visit. As I was getting my mom ready to see the nurse it was time for her to get changed. Mom said to me "I think I stinky," but she didn't say stinky she said another word, lol. I said "okay" but as I began to remove her diaper it was filled with a lot of black poop. I said, "Hold on Ma, don't move!" She agreed, so I ran downstairs to get a lot of plastic grocery bags, more wipes, and clothes. The doorbell rang it was the nurse. When I told her what was going on she said, "Okay, let's get her cleaned up." She really helped me get her cleaned up! It was a lot of work, but I didn't care. I was making sure she was going to be taken care of. My mom laid still until we were finished and felt much better after we were done. I asked the nurse why it looked like that; she told me in so many words that it was her last bowel movement. I was in a state of shock! I had never experience anything like this. I had never been a caregiver, only God gave me the strength to take care of her and not get agitated and upset about it. I did the best I could to take care of her.

Since it was Thanksgiving, I wanted to get out for a while. My Aunt Mary came over and sat with my mom while I went to my friend's house for Thanksgiving Day. Before my mom's health started failing, she was wanted to go to my friend's house to eat Thanksgiving, too. She said that she hoped she could make it up their steps, basically their porch but my mom was in no condition to go anywhere so my Aunt Mary came over and I left to go spend some time with my friends. I had a good time but the whole time my mind was wondering how my mom was doing, so I kept checking up on her to make sure she was doing alright. When I got back home my other aunt was there too. She told me that my mom kept trying to take off her shirt. She kept saying that she was hot and they had to fight with her so she wouldn't take it off. I said, "Ma you can't lay here with your boobs out!" I ended up cracking the window so she could get some air and cool off. After my family left, I got my mom settled for bed so she could rest and I could as well, but once again I was up throughout the night because I was able to hear her on the baby monitor. I had to get up to give her more pain meds so she could rest and not be in pain.

November 27, 2015

My middle daughter Nadia's birthday is on this day and she was so happy that my mom was still alive on her day. That morning I told my mom it was Nadia's birthday, she said, "is it?" I assured her and called Nadia on the phone so my mom could talk to her. I had to put my headphones in her ear and held the phone for her so she could talk to her. I'm not sure what Nadia was saying to her, but I heard my mom say, "Nadia you know I can't run behind him right now." I knew she had to be talking about my grandson Kamryn. She also told Nadia "You is still talk too much" I started laughing because I figured Nadia was getting on her nerves.

After they finished, my dad came by to sit with my mom because I had to go take Nadia to work. My mom said to my dad "Glenn where is my $2.00 at?" My daddy said "What? I don't have your $.2.00!" My mom said again to my daddy, "Where is my $2.00 at Glenn?" My daddy started getting mad, until I explained to him that was how she had begun speaking as of recent. He was okay after that - he couldn't understand why she was asking him that so thankfully I was there to explain. My mom and daddy would fuss at each other all the time. They would have heated arguments all the time. I believe my mom was still upset with my dad for breaking her heart when I was younger. My mom and dad got married and on the same day he married her, he left her that night. My mom was so broken about it. In spite of what he did, my daddy would do anything for her. It didn't matter what she needed he always provided. He would give her rides to work on some days when it was too cold or too hot outside for her to catch the city bus back and forth to work. I hated being in between their arguments, though. I would stay out of it because I knew once they made it up everything was alright between them. I waited patiently for those moments.

November 28, 2015

Time Has Drawn Near

It was Saturday morning and I had to work, from at 8:30am-5:00pm. I got up to do my usually routine, give my mom her medicine and change her, but this morning she felt warm to me as if she had a fever. I checked her temperature it was 102. I read the guide book the hospice nurse gave me. In the book stated that I could give her some Tylenol, so I went to Family Dollar to get the medicine. She wasn't responding to me, so I gave her the Tylenol thru a syringe, since that was the only way she was able to take it. I put a cold rag on her forehead and neck to cool her down and called hospice to let them know what was going on. The nurse told me to see what happens when I give her the Tylenol and for me to call them back. Since I had to work, I asked my Uncle James to come over to sit with my mom.

While I was working, I felt heavy and I cried all morning. Then, I got an unexpected call from my friend Monifa. She said that while she was asleep, the Lord told her to call me, so she did. I told her everything that was going on with my mom; she couldn't believe she was that sick. She gave me her mom's number so I could call her but, I didn't get a chance to do so. After I got off the phone with Monifa,

I checked my mom's temperature - it was going down some but not that much, so I gave her some more Tylenol. My Uncle James was talking on the phone with a family member, who gave him the phone number to call an Evangelist to come over to see my mom and do prayer. She came over she saw my mom just sleeping. She had some anointing oil and communion with her. She put the anointing oil on my mom's head, began to pray, and we did communion. My mom wasn't responding to me at all, but I was able to get her to do communion. I had to wet the cracker a little bit so it could be softer since she couldn't chew it and I used a straw to scoop out the juice so I could put it on her tongue; she started making sucking movements with her mouth. She would not drink anything all day but was alert enough to do the communion. The Evangelist said,

"I've done all that I could do and when God says enough is enough that's when it will be."

I cried some more as she and my Uncle James left. I cried and cried as I knew the end was drawing near but didn't know exactly when. My Uncle Tight called me and said he wanted to come by to see her. I told him that it was okay, since they were very close and I knew he was concerned about her. One of my mom's friends came by too, but I told her my mom was too sick to have visitors. My Uncle Tight came by with his friends; they were close to my mom and would hang out together. When they saw the state my mom was in, it was hard for them to bare it. They were in disbelief and my Uncle Tight just cried. I never seen him so emotional - he is always tough and strong, but this situation regarding my mom was too much on his heart for him to bare. One of their friends told me that my mom told him that she knew that the cancer was going to take her out, but she was going to live her life. He told me they walked to the store, bought beers, and sat on her porch and talked and laughed.

Once my uncle and his friends left, I called my best friend Angie. I told her about my mom while I cried and cried. I knew my mom's health was changing for the worst. Without hesitation, Angie came right over. I called Hospice back to see if a nurse could come over to check my mom out to see what is going on. I felt like at this moment it will be best if she went into a hospice facility, so she could get better care. My friend Netta was coming by with her son Jason to pick up her scarf she had left at the hair salon; they arrived at my house at the same time. We went upstairs to the room my mom was in. Suddenly, my mom tried to sit up and said, "I got to throw up." I ran and got a towel and ask Netta and Jason to help me sit her up. Once we got her up, she threw up a huge blood clot. I said, "That's it, I'm calling 911!" When I called, I had to give them my mom's medical history. I had to lock my house up and I was able to ride in the ambulance with her in the front seat. There was a DNR, otherwise known as "Do not resuscitate," on file. I was heartbroken when my mom signed the DNR form because I wanted to save her life, keep her on life support etc. My mom told me she didn't want me to have to go through the pressure of having to decide to take her off life support if something happened to her. She knew as a mother that would be too much from me to handle, so she just wanted to go peacefully. I was told trying to resuscitate her in her condition could cause more damage than good as her ribs would be crushed and she would be in a lot of pain.

Once we got to the hospital my family and friends came over. I showed the nurse what was in the towel. The nurse said that it wasn't a good sign and I had to make a choice to either have her body go through more agony by having more tests run or just let her rest and see what happens. I finally said to the doctor that my mom has endured enough. My family saw her in the emergency room, as the chaplain came by to talk to me before she was taken upstairs to a room. I had left out to go talk to my family and friends that were in the waiting area to update them on my mom's condition. Once I came back in, Diesha told me that my mom said,

"I will be okay."

I hate I didn't get a chance to hear her say that. That was last time she spoke. I told my son Quan to come in to see her because that may be the last time he would see her alive. I told him he didn't have to stay long; he only stayed for about a minute then he walked out. I know he doesn't accept it when bad things happen to well, and I understood what he was going through. I told everyone to leave out of the room so I could talk to my mom. She was moved up to her room, as my family and friends began leaving. My Uncle James and my friend Lin (Nu Nu Aunt) stayed with me. We had to stand outside of the room while the nurses get her settled in.

My mom had on a pink shirt; some of the communion juice spilled on the collar of the shirt. I made sure I grabbed it so I could keep it after she was dressed into the hospital gown. Once we got in the room, my mom was laying there sleeping with Morphine drip medication being given to her. I played a video that was in my cell phone of her singing her favorite song by John Legend called "Who Do We Think We Are." In the video, she was just singing with her cigarette in her hand, as happy as could be. I cried and Lin hugged me. I played the song for her I put my earphones in her ear. I was told your hearing is the last thing you lose before you pass away.

My cousin Alex came by to see her, too. I was shocked because his mom passed away when he was teenager. My mom and his mom are sisters (My Aunt Diane). We all just sat there quietly, sleeping off and on as the nurses would come in throughout the night checking on my mom's vital signs. Lin sat up and slept in a single chair that was in the room. The support I received was overwhelming, my heart was filled with joy.

The End of the Journey

November 29, 2015

I woke up the next morning. Lin, my Uncle James, and I went downstairs to the cafeteria to go get some breakfast. After we ate, Lin laid down on the bench chair that was in the room; once she laid there, she finally got some better sleep and rest. One of my mom's doctors came by; she treated my mom whenever my mom had hospital stays. When she walked in the room, I burst out crying and she gave me the biggest hug My mom didn't like talking to her because has a strong accent. My mom couldn't really understand what she was saying, so I would have to translate for her. I was so happy she came by to see about us.

My Uncle James and Lin finally went home. My sister came by, though I was not expecting to see her. She told me that my dad told her what was going on and she needed to come and see me. I am my mom's only child, and she is my sister by my dad, but she stayed with me the whole time. More family members came by, so I decided to go home to get some clothes and freshen up. I packed my duffle bag because I was going to stay at the hospital with my mom for however long I needed to - I was not leaving her side. I was told that usually a person won't pass away while their loved ones are present. I told my family while I'm gone, they better call me ASAP if something changes. I hurried home and got my pillow and blanket and some clothes. I hurried back to the hospital, I walked into the room, and she was still alive. I felt relieved. We all just sat around and talked and laughed. The nurses came in to make sure she was changed and to give her Morphine to keep her comfortable. Whenever they would come in, I noticed she was alert a little bit, so I took every opportunity that I could get to talk to her. There came a moment when I asked everybody to step out for a minute, so I could have some private time with her. I started talking to her by holding her face close to mine. I knew she could hear me. I said to her,

"I love you and you were a good mommy to me. I will be okay, God got me! I will make sure Nu Nu is taking care of. I will be alright, I'll be okay."

Her face bumped my face. I knew she heard me. As she mumbled as if she was trying to say something back to me, no words came out of her mouth. I hugged her. I do believe she was trying to tell me she loved me back. I'm glad to know that she heard me, she knew I was there, and she was not alone. Everybody came back in. I sat in the chair beside her and held her hand the entire time, thinking back on that day, most people take pictures of holding their loved one's hand. I hated to even fathom that picture being ours soon.

My Ex-Mother In-law came by to see me and support me. I was happy to see her. I was shocked to see her and was not expecting to see her but knew that my ex-husband told her what was going on since were texting from time to time. She told me what to expect because she had been this type of situations before. She stayed for a little while, then left. It was about 6:00 when the nurse came in to check on my mom. She advised it was no point of keeping her on the oxygen because she was not breathing thru her nose, she was mainly breathing thru her mouth. The oxygen was unplugged but my mom kept on breathing. The nurse told us that when she was starting to come close to death, she would have white spots on her legs but so far, we didn't see any. She also advised us of the "death rattle," but so far, she was quiet.

My Uncle James, Diesha and my sister were still in the room with me. Lin called me and told me she was on her way back to the hospital. I told everyone that my mom was waiting on Nu Nu and told Lin to bring Nu Nu when she came back. I called Nadia's boyfriend and had him to put KamRyn, my grandson, on the phone so my mom could hear his voice so he could talk to her. He said "Hey Nanna! I love you Nanna." Once Nu Nu got there, my mom started talking and laughing. Suddenly, my mom started breathing hard and fast. I called for the nurse to come back in, she listened to my mom's heart she asked,

"Did somebody new come into the room. What new voice did she hear?"

I said my granddaughter. I had Lin to take Nu Nu out of the room. I didn't want her to see what was going on. I put my hand on my mom's chest and began telling her to calm down; I had no idea that this was the actual transition state. The nurse left out to go get some more medicine. She was still breathing fast but it was starting to slow down. I started playing gospel songs for her and put my phone close to her pillow. The first song I played was "Let the Church Say Amen." Her breathing started to slow down some more. I put my face to her face so she could hear me tell her I loved her and that I was going to miss her. At that moment, I knew God gave me the strength to be able to allow the process of her dying without breaking down screaming, hollering, and crying. I played another song called "Jesus" by Dorothy Norwood, and "Awesome God" by Brian Courtney Wilson. She was really calm, but her breathing was different. I played the last song called "God Is Trying to Tell You Something" from The Color Purple Movie since that song was her favorite one. I still had my face close to her face. My sister was rubbing my back and gently whispered,

"It's time to let her go."

I was singing to her. The song went off and the room was quiet. I lifted my head up and she was still and quiet, no movement from her chest at all, no noise, no breathing absolutely nothing. We were like "Oh God, that's it?" I looked up at the clock it was 8:48pm. She passed away so peacefully, we didn't realize it because she was so quiet. I called the nurse to come back in to check her vital signs. She told me that her heartbeat was fainting and that she could not hear it. I told Lin to bring Nu Nu back in.

"Your Nannie is an Angel now."

"Her body is here but she's an Angel in heaven?"

"Yes."

I didn't cry. God gave me the strength to stay strong for Nu Nu, I could not let her see my upset because I did not want her upset. I started calling my family and friends to let them know my mom passed away. My friends came over. I called Quan and Nadia and told them, Nadia came on over as soon as she got off work, and as soon as she walked into the room, she cried so bad. Once Nadia cried Diesha started to cry too, Diesha tried to maintain her cry because she was pregnant but she couldn't hold it another moment. I still had to hold myself together for them. The nurse came in and started taking the bands off my mom's wrist. She had a "Fall Risk" band on and an ID band on. I asked her if I could have them, she told me "yes."

I propped my mom's head up on her pillow so her head would be balanced. I took pictures of her, Nu Nu took a picture with her; she was smiling, she was doing good. My mom looked so peaceful and sleep. Nadia told Nu Nu that her Nannie loved her. As soon as she spoke those words to Nu Nu with tears streaming down her face, Nu Nu cried, too. She cried so hard and loud. Her cousin had to pick her up and take her out of the room. We all could hear her in the hallway crying until she got on the elevator. I called to check up on her and she was still crying when they got her into the car. I told Nadia she should've kept quiet because we didn't want Nu Nu to get upset. It was so emotional for everybody and we were so heartbroken. Me? I was numb about what had just happened. My mom died and I was so calm about it. I know that it was only God, and He kept me through it all. If he didn't step in, I would've broken down terribly. I was

94

her only child and had never experienced the death of someone who takes their last breath before.

I asked everybody to leave out so I could say my final goodbyes to my mom and to spend some time with her alone. I started packing up my stuff. I grabbed her hand, I just shouted from the top of my lungs. I said: THANK YOU, THANK YOU LORD, THANK YOU, THANK YOU LORD, THANK YOU, THANK YOU LORD, THANK YOU LORD!! As I was walking out of the room, I believe I heard a voice in my head say, "don't leave." Thinking back, that is the only regret that I have is that I didn't stay until the funeral home came and got her. I was by her side the whole time. I drove myself home and got settled. I couldn't say anything; I was still trying to process the fact that my mom died. All I could do was lay down and go to sleep.

I had a dream that my mom was at a doctor's office. He had on a white jacket, with a clipboard in his hand. Three women were with us, one of them was my mom and the other two were like sisters. My mom had a head full of hair and it was on her shoulders. The doctor told my mom to run up and down the hallway. As she was running, there were some people standing her in way. She got mad and told them to move out of her way. By the time she ran back to where the doctor was standing with a clip board in his hand, he told her

"Nobody has been able to run like that.

You did a good job!"

After The Journey

A few days went by I had to make arrangements at the funeral home; my mom wanted to be cremated. She would often joke and say, "Don't spend a lot of money putting me in the ground, just put me in a box with some jeans and tennis shoes on." She loved her jeans and tennis shoes; now don't get me wrong, she would wear cute dresses too, but my mom loved dressing comfortably. If she didn't feel comfortable, she would change her clothes all throughout the day until she felt right. In the mornings when she would get dressed for work, clothes would be everywhere spread across her bed until she found something she really liked to wear.

While I was making the arrangements, the funeral director advised me that my mom was there at the facility. I started crying, and the director notice I was getting teary eyed. She handed me some tissue. I said,

"She is here now?"

She said, "yes." My heart was aching so bad, I had to take a moment to get myself together so I could finish completing the arrangements. My Uncle James and my Aunt Mary (Uncle James' Wife) went with me to help me get things in order. I saw this pretty pink Urn that was sitting on the shelf that I picked out to have her remains put in. I asked if my mom would be cremated in the blue hospital gown and those yellow soft slip resistant socks? She said yes. I said "Oh no! I will bring her something to wear. I do not want to see my mom for the last time in that blue hospital gown and those yellow socks before she was cremated."

I gathered her life insurance paperwork together and finalized everything. The date was set for me and few of my family members to do a final viewing. I went out and got her pretty white laced dress and I went to the Breast Cancer store on State Street and found her a cute cap to go on her head. I got some pink pearls and earrings and of course some other cute soft pink socks to go on her feet. I dropped of her belongings to the funeral home. I wanted to make sure my last viewing of my mother was going to be a good memory.

I was able to see her looking dressed up like she always was. The next day we were able to see her. She looked so pretty and at peace. My Aunt Pam said she looked like their mother laying there. I took pictures of her. I touched her. I touched her breast. I could still feel the lump. My Daddy made me angry; he kept saying, "It don't look like her! It most definitely don't look like her." I was so furious with my daddy by the comment he made. I ended up saying to him "SO WHAT it's still her, this is still my mother!" He noticed that I was upset with him by the tone of my voice. I've never been disrespectful or spoke out of tone to my daddy but that day, he made me upset, he ended up apologizing to me for his comment. Her appearance did change a little, but I knew it was her. Even though I didn't want my mother to be cremated, looking back I am glad she was, because I did not want to hear people whispering about her appearance if they would have seen her laying in a casket. She looked beautiful! She did not look ugly or unrecognizable, but she did look a little different than her normal self.

As I prepared myself to leave the funeral home, I was okay, but I was still in disbelief that my mother passed away, I was still in shock. The funeral director did ask if I wanted to be there when they cremated her but I said, "No I don't want to be here knowing what you all are doing to her in the back room." I advised her to call me when she was ready to be picked up. My mental would have not been able to handle that at all.

When I got the call that her remains were ready, my Uncle James and I went to go pick her up. I had them to seal her urn because I did not trust my children (well only Nadia because she would've been curious and would want to open the Urn to see what it looks like. What if somehow an accident happened and her ashes fell out, what would I do then, so to save my sanity I had her Urn top sealed.

I decided to have a memorial service for her at my church. I had T-Shirts made with her picture on it and her birth date and death date. I had them made for myself and my family and they turned out cute! (We still wear them from time to time. I only wear my shirt on her birthday and the date she passed away.) My Mother's memorial service went well. I had her urn and a picture of her and a Breast Cancer balloon on the table as the set up in front of the church with a pink tablecloth. As my family and I walked in some of my extended family was there along with some friends, especially my mom's close friends. A video slide of her was presented as the song "Heaven Waits for Me" played. We all pretty much handled things, well, as best we good. We had repast at the church for the family only, but we also had another repast at my house where more of the family and my friends came over. We did a balloon release from there. As we wrote on the balloons, we prayed, released them, and cried some more. I prayed with tears in my eyes saying, "One day soon a cure would be discovered, and more lives would be saved from this awful disease that is taking people's lives!" Nu Nu said a few words as well. As I cried, a rainbow appeared. Someone told me that the Lord was pleased and my mother was alright. I knew what they said was true but I could not stop the tears. I cried some more. I wanted her here with me not gone away from me. I was taken away from my mother when I was three years old and now, she was taken away from me again. I knew her body was tired, and she needed rest.

God gave me the strength to let her go and let rest and get the healing she deserved to have on the other side. I wished her healing could have taken place here but that was not the plan God had for her life. He gave her **REST**, he gave her wonderful **REST**, he gave her joyous **REST**. As I look back on her life, He was with her through it all. She knew that He was there. God had her and she fought and endured all the way to end, until she couldn't fight any more; at that moment, she surrendered and took a sigh of relief. Now, she can **REST**.

In the end God is God. I had to accept what God allowed, and He gave me the strength to do so. As my former Pastor said "Tracy, God is going to give you the strength to endure what is about to happen." I didn't quite take in what he was saying but I knew it was about my mother.

My Mother missed out on seven years of my life because I was taken from her at the age of three. She was given seven years to be a Great grandmother to my granddaughter, Nu Nu. God has a way that is mighty, mighty, sweet.

I asked my mother one day,

"Ma the way you take care of Nu Nu if you were given the chance, you would have taken care of me like that?'

She said, "Yes," and got teary-eyed. I saw the bond my mother and Nu Nu had. I never tried come between their relationship even though Nu Nu was my granddaughter and my mother was her Great-Grandmother. I understood the bond they had; for some reason, God only knows why their bond was so close. It was as if he gave my mother back the 7 years, she didn't have with me, she experienced with Nu Nu.

I give God all the Glory and Honor and Praise; he is just that good and kind!

I asked my mother before her health got bad if she felt that I was upset with her for not taking care of me when I was younger? She began to cry and she "Yes" I told her I was never upset with her, I always wanted to be with her. I never threw it up in her face and said, "You didn't take care of me, you wasn't there for me." I never said those things to her. I was told one thing about my childhood as to why she couldn't take care of me, but I also knew she had a story was well. The things she told me, I understood. I also understood the side that I was told as well. Again, as I mentioned before when the time was right for me to go back to live with my mother, she did her best to provide for me. She did the best she could; she worked and made sure I ate. I never went to bed hungry! We didn't always have heat and lights on all the time but she did her best.

She was the BEST Mom ever.

I was her only child! She loved me and I knew it. She would say I was spoiled! She would always say to me,

"I cannot have 2 of you!" lol.

Indeed, she was, the best Mom, ever.

It is Well

My mom endured a lot in her lifetime but would always fight her way through it. She was physically abused, and verbally abused by the men she dated. She was a tough woman that did not tolerate foolishness from people; life events made her that way. She was loyal to her family and friends but also protective of us all. My mom didn't raise me all my life. I lived with my great aunt from the time I was three years old until I was ten years old.

My mom always loved my dad. She would always hope that they would be together some day, but my dad wouldn't act right, therefore, they remained friends. She did the best she could to take care of me despite of many obstacles she had to face to take care of me. She didn't attend church all the time, but I know she believed in the Lord Our Savior, Christ Jesus. She was an awesome grandmother to my children. All my children loved her.

Through the trials and tribulations, we both endured, it was always God, My Mom, and I.

"Honor (respect, obey, care for) your father and your mother, so that your days may be prolonged in the land the LORD your God gives you."

Exodus 20:12 (AMP)

Connect with the Author

Tracy R. Eleazer a native of Greensboro, North Carolina. She is a single mother of three, Diesha, Nadia and Yuquan and a grandmother of seven and four bonus grandchildren. She is the founder and C.E.O. of Creations by "Tracy," a company was established January 14, 2013. She also serves as a Minister in Training at Tabernacle of Meeting also located in Greensboro, North Carolina.

Tracy is an author who writes nonfiction books that provide details of personal events that have occurred in her life. Her first book, <u>God My Mom & I</u>, is a story of her mother's battle with Stage Four Breast Cancer. Through this first release, it is her hope to inspire people and share the importance of early detection.

www.ingramcontent.com/pod-product-compliance
Lightning Source LLC
LaVergne TN
LVHW051700080426
835511LV00017B/2643